THE POETRY WORKSHOP

ASHOK JAHAGIRDAR

Made with ♥ on the Notion Press Platform
www.notionpress.com

For the dreamers who turn whispers into verse,

the broken-hearted who mend themselves with metaphors,

and the quiet observers who find poetry in the ordinary.

For the teachers who handed me pencils,

the friends who lent me their ears,

and the strangers who became muses.

This is for the workshop of life -

where every stumble is a stanza,

every silence, a line waiting to be written.

Contents

Preface

"The Poetry Workshop" is not just a collection of poem - it is an invitation. An invitation to wander through the raw, unpolished corridors of thought where words stumble, rise, and sometimes dance. These pages are not filled with perfect verses, but with the messy, beautiful process of creation itself.

I did not write this book alone. It was shaped by late-night conversations with fellow writers, by the quiet hum of coffee shops where ink met paper, and by the unspoken stories of strangers who passed through my life like fleeting stanzas. Some poems arrived fully formed, gifts from some unseen muse. Others were wrestled onto the page, reshaped a dozen times, and still bear the scars of their making.

This is not a manual on how to write poetry. It is a testament to why we "need" to—to untangle the knots within us, to name the unnameable, to find communion in shared silence. Here, you'll find love letters and laments, questions without answers, and fragments that refuse to be finished. Some pieces will whisper to you; others may leave you unsettled. That, too, is part of the work.

To the reader: May you find in these lines a mirror or a doorway. And if you've ever felt the urge to pick up a pen, may this book be the nudge you need. The workshop is always open.

This is not the end of the conversation—only the beginning.

Acknowledgements

Gratitude to mentors, fellow poets, friends, and family who inspired, critiqued, and supported this collection.

The author, though by profession is a Tutor (Information Technology), he is passionate about poetry.

In this collection, the poem that the poet he looks on with pride is "**The Raven's Quill.**"

"**The Raven's Quill**" explores the interplay between memory and myth, framed through the metaphor of a raven's flight as an inky stroke across the sky. inspired by the natural and supernatural, The poet has sought to bridge the eerie and the elegant, using rhythm and metaphor to evoke both unease and wonder. **"The Raven's Quill" i**s particularly dear to him because "**it was born from a midnight walk under starless sky, where the silence itself felt like a a language",** - but he admits that the seeds for "**The Raven's Quill**" were sown when , many, many years earlier he had the opportunity to read some of the works of the legendary writer Edgar Allan Poe.

1. How to Build a Poem (A meta-poem about the messy process of writing)

Start with the fracture -
the splintered thing lodged in your ribs
that no cough can dislodge.
Call it "inspiration" if you must,
but know it is just hunger
with a prettier name.
Next, the bones:
a rhythm tapped absentmindedly
on a diner table,
the half-heard melody
of a stranger's laugh,
the way your childhood home
still hums in your teeth
when you say its name.
Now, the bloodwork -
verbs writhing like minnows in your palms,
adjectives that stick like burrs to your sleeves.
(Here is where you'll bleed.
A poem is not a wound,
but the salt rubbed into one.)

Arrange the fragments on the page.
Watch them refuse to fit.
This is the part where you learn:
a poem is not a puzzle,
but the hand that shakes
as it forces the pieces together.
Finally, the lie -
the smoothing, the sanding,
the pretense that this
was always the shape
you intended.
Sign your name at the bottom.
Walk away before it cracks.

2. The Workshop (On the vulnerability of sharing unfinished art)

We gather like surgeons
in a theatre of light,
our pens scalpels,
our notebooks sterile fields.
"Consider cutting the third stanza,"
someone suggests,
and I nod as if my ribs
aren't splayed open on the table.
Across the room, a woman reads
a poem about her father's hands.
Her voice splinters on the word *work*.
We offer our critiques like breadcrumbs,
pretending we are not also
starving.
This is the sacred paradox:
we come to fix the broken things,
but the breaking is the point.
Every "I don't understand this line"
is a confession:
I, too, have been misunderstood.

When the last page is folded shut,

we linger,

cradling our coffees like excuses.

No one admits

we are not here to polish poems,

but to prove

we are not alone

in our unmaking.

3. What the River Taught Me (On revision, impermanence, and letting go)

The river does not apologize

for the stones it grinds to dust,

for the banks it reshapes in the night.

It does not beg forgiveness

for the dead branches

it carries like unread letters

to the sea.

I, too, am learning

to love the wreckage

of my first drafts -

the lines drowned in red ink,

the metaphors bloated

as drowned things,

the stanzas I once loved

now sunk in the silt of better choices.

I am learning to kneel

at the water's edge,

to dip my hands in

and drink the cold proof
that movement is not betrayal,
that change is the only way
to remain alive.
(Do not mistake this for surrender.
Even the river fights
when it meets the ocean.)

4. Literary Devices

"Simile" raises her hand

"Likea mothto a flame" is overused—

Try "Likea librarian to a mishelved book"

Or **"Like a ghost to its own echo."***

"Metaphor" Crosses His Arms:

Why say "your eyes are stars"

When they are clearly

The last two lights in a blackout,

The ones that flicker

just *before* the power returns?

"Enjambment" Sighs:

Your lines are so obedient,

Always ending where expected.

Let them spill. Let them

Trip down the stairs of the page.

The Poet Whispers:

But what if they see

How badly I want this?

"Personification" Smirks:

Exactly.

5. How to build a poem (2)

"Gather Your Tools"

A blank page is not empty—

It hums with the static of unwritten words.

Take your pen (or your trembling fingers)

And puncture the silence.

"Measure the Silence"

Every poem begins in the negative space—

Count the heartbeats between "I" and "love"

And "you." The unsaid is your first stanza.

"Mix Metaphors Carelessly"

Let the river of your thoughts

Crash into the bakery of your memories.

Yes, the oven is a sun.

Yes, the dough is your kneaded childhood.

No, you cannot burn the water.

"Sand Down the Edges"

A poem is not a polished stone

But the grit in your shoe

That makes you limp beautifully.

Keep the awkward lines—

they are the fingerprints

of your reaching.

"The Ghost of the First Draft"

It will haunt you.

That one line you deleted—

"Her laughter was a key turning in the lock"—

will rattle its chains at 3 a.m.

"Do not exorcise it."

Feed it sugar cubes of what-ifs.

Let it sleep at the foot of your bed.

All poems are built on burial grounds.

"Erasure as Resurrection"

Black out the words that don't tremble.

What's left will be a skeleton

dancing in the margins.

"Try it:"

Take a newspaper headline—

War Declared, Markets Fall -

and carve a love poem from the wreckage:

Declared: / fall / into me.

"The Workshop critiques in your heart"

Too sentimental,"* says the man in the corduroy blazer.

"Try less blood next time."

"The metaphor on line seven is unstable,"

says the woman who has never

balanced a teacup on her sternum.

"Nod politely."

Then go home and write the poem

that would make them blush.

"Send It Into the World"

Tuck it into a bottle.

Release it into the subway's underground river.

Let it be the graffiti that outlasts the wall.

Or:

Fold it into a paper airplane.

Aim for the open window of a passing car.

Hope the driver is lonely.

Or:

Whisper it to the dogwood tree.

Let the wind decide.

"Repeat Until Death"

You will run out of ink.

You will run out of time.

The last poem you ever write

will be half-finished,

and that's okay.

6. The Raven's Quill

The Invocation

Beneath the pallid moon's unblinking stare,
Where shadows coil like serpents in the air,
I dip my quill in ink of midnight hue,
And summon verse as Poe himself once knew.
Oh, Muse of Murmurs, wraith of woeful song,
Who guides lost poets through the dark too long,
Lend me your ear—this chant of woe and wit,
A thousand words where spectral meanings sit.

The Descent

The cellar door creaks on its rusted hinge,
A sound that lingers like a whispered cringe.
Down, down I step, where candlelight is weak,
And every sigh becomes a phantom's shriek.
The walls are lined with books of tattered skin,
Their leather cracked, their secrets locked within.
Each title glows in gilt now worn with age—

The Ghoul's Lament, The Madman's Rage.
A raven perches on a bust of yore,
Its beak agape as though it craves one more
Dark stanza spun from nightmares half-remembered,
Or sins too foul for daylight to surrender.

The Workshop

Here, spectres gather in a ghastly throng,
Their hollow eyes demanding mournful song.
A woman wreathed in mist recites her verse,
Her voice a knell, her cadence like a curse:
"The clock struck twelve, `yet time stood still,
Upon the hill where blood did spill.
The dead arose in lace and bone,
To claim the hearts they once had known."
A gentleman in rot-stitched velvet bows,
Then reads his lines with voice like scraping ploughs:
"The mirror shows not what is there,
But vacant eyes and matted hair.
A face not mine—yet oh, too true—
It grins and mouths, 'I remember you.'"

The Craft

The Raven croaks, "Nevermore the lie,
That poetry must soothe or beautify.

True verse should haunt, should twist, should cling,

Like ivy slow-throttling a king."

I take my pen—its nib a dagger's edge—

And carve my soul upon the parchment's ledge.

Each metaphor a razor's kiss,

Each rhyme a footfall in the abyss.

"The lover's touch was cold as snow,

Her lips the shade of mistletoe.

Yet when she spoke, her breath was flame -

And thus I learned to love the pain."

The spectres nod; the air grows thick.

The Raven's eyes are candlewick—

Two burning coals that sear my sight,

As shadows coil in verse and bite.

The Revelation

A thousand words? A paltry sum,

When weighed against the deafening hum

Of voices lost, of souls undone,

Who trade their peace for parlous pun.

Yet as I write, the walls dissolve,

The workshop fades, the ghosts absolve

Their debts to time—and one by one,

They vanish where the moon has shone.

The Raven spreads his wings so wide,

They blot the stars, then subside.

"The poem's done," he bids me know,
"Yet still its echoes fester… Go."

The Farewell

I close the book. The cellar's cold.
The candle's dead. The tale is told.
Yet in my ears, the whispers play -
The workshop's chant won't fade away.
And so I leave this crypt of thought,
With every line in shadow wrought.
A thousand words? Perhaps. But more—
For poetry knocks at Death's dark door.

7. The Blank Page

The blank page is an open field,
white as winter, vast and yield-
less until the plow of pen
carves its furrows, now and then.
I stare into the emptiness,
a wilderness of wordlessness,
where silence hums a quiet tune,
a hollow, haunting kind of moon.
What shall I plant in this pale earth?
Seeds of sorrow? Songs of mirth?
Roots of rage or vines of love,
twisting upward, toward the sun?
The first mark is the hardest stroke—
a crack in ice, the faintest smoke
rising from an unborn fire,
a whisper, not yet a choir.
But once the letters start to dance,
the page no longer wears a trance.
Ink bleeds into thirsty threads,
a garden growing from my head.
And yet, the fear is always near—
what if the words just disappear?
What if the lines collapse like sand,

slipping through my trembling hand?
But still, I write. I must. I do.
The blank page waits, expectant, true.
A mirror, first—then, if I'm wise,
a window. Then, a pair of eyes

8. The Poet's Bones

The poet's bones are made of verse,
fragile, strong, and sometimes terse.
Each rib a stanza, curved and tight,
the spine a line that stands upright.
The skull—a sonnet, dense and round,
where all the brightest thoughts are found.
The fingers, slender metaphors,
tapping on life's hidden doors.
But poets, too, are flesh and blood,
prone to silence, prone to flood.
They starve, they feast, they laugh, they weep,
they wake the world, or let it sleep.
Some days, the words flow like a river,
a silver tongue, a constant shiver.
Other days, the well is dry,
just echoes in a hollow sky.
And when the poet's bones grow old,
when ink runs pale and hands are cold,
will the poems linger on,
long after breath and voice are gone?
Or will they fade like footprints left
in shifting sands, of meaning bereft?
No matter—still, the poet writes,

to cast their soul in black and whites.
For even if the world forgets,
the poet knows—no true word dies.
It only sleeps in someone's eyes,
until they wake it, by surprise.

9. The Workshop

We sit in a circle of chairs and doubt,
each clutching words we've carved out
from the caves of our chests, raw and rough,
hoping the others won't call our bluff.
"I like the imagery here," one voice will say,
"But maybe cut the third stanza—it's in the way."
Another will murmur, *"The rhythm's off beat,"
while someone else sighs, *"But the ending's sweet."
We dissect our darlings with surgical hands,
trimming the fat, tightening bands.
A metaphor's mangled, a simile's saved,
a line's resurrected from its grammatical grave.
And yet, beneath the critique and the craft,
there's something unspoken, something daft—
a shared delirium, a silent vow,
to chase the ghost of the 'right word' now.
For what is a workshop but a forge of thought,
where poems are hammered, burned, and wrought?
Where voices tremble, then rise again,
stronger for having been broken, then.
And when we leave, our pages marked,
with scribbles, cuts, and question marks,
we know the truth: the poem's not done.

It's only just begun.

10. For the Soil That Made Me

The air is thick with smoke and screams,
the earth is trembling, split at seams.
My brothers fall like autumn wheat,
scythed down by death's unfeeling heat.
I clutch my rifle, slick with grime,
each breath a labor, each step a climb.
The sky is bleeding crimson hues,
a mirror of the hell we choose.
"Hold the line!" the sergeant roars,
but half his voice is lost to wars
that swallow men like shifting sands—
no time for prayers, no time for hands
to close their eyes or say the words
that mothers hum to restless birds.
To my left, a boy of nineteen gasps,
his uniform a flood of scraps.
His fingers clutch a fading thread—
a photograph, now streaked with red.
"Tell her - " he starts, but silence stays.
Another name the wind will raise.
I want to kneel. I want to weep.
But duty is a fire I keep

alive inside my hollow chest,
where love and terror both contest.
I think of home—the fields I knew,
the golden dawn, the morning dew
on petals bending in the breeze,
the laughter dancing through the trees.
My mother's hands, rough yet kind,
pressing bread she'd barely find
into my pack. "Come back * she'd said,
her eyes two wells of tears unshed.
The cannons boom. The ground erupts.
Another soul is briefly cupped
by hands unseen, then left to fade
into the mud the shells have made.
I do not fight for kings or crowns,
for politicians' hollow sounds.
I do not fight for glory's claim,
a footnote in some distant name.
I fight because the soil remembers
the footsteps of my past Decembers,
the rivers where I learned to swim,
the hymns we sang at twilight's rim.
I fight because the wind still carries
the voice of those the war unwarranted.
I fight because the land is mine -
not by deed, but by the line
of sweat and blood and whispered dreams

that stitch the earth with unseen seams.
A bullet grazes. Blood runs warm.
I do not stop. I press on, torn
between the living and the dead,
between the screams and words unsaid.
If I must fall, let it be
where my last sight is sky and tree,
where my last breath is not a cry,
but one more whisper to the sky:
" tried. I fought. For you, I stood.
For you, my motherland—my blood."

Gratitude to mentors, fellow poets, friends, and family who inspired, critiqued, and supported this collection.